The Life Cycle of an Apple Tree

Over and Over Again

Gillian Clifto..

COMPUTER SCIENCE For the REAL World™

Rosen Classroom™

Published in 2018 by The Rosen Publishing Group, Inc.
29 East 21st Street, New York, NY 10010

Book Design: Jennifer Ryder-Talbot
Editor: Caitie McAneney

Photo Credits: Cover CorneliaP/Shutterstock.com; p. 4 Smileus/ Shutterstock.com; p. 4 (seed) Sutichak/Shutterstock.com; p. 6 hacohob/ Shutterstock.com; p. 8 Gina Rothfels/ Shutterstock.com; p. 10 tankist276/ Shutterstock.com; p. 12 Behling/Shutterstock.com; p. 14 Designua/Shutterstock.com.

ISBN: 9781538352434
6-pack ISBN: 9781508136910

Manufactured in the United States of America

CPSIA Compliance Information: Batch #WS18RC: For Further Information contact Rosen Publishing, New York, New York at 1-800-237-9932

Table of Contents

Life Cycle Loops 5

Starting as a Seed 7

Sprout to Seedling 9

Growing Taller 11

Dropping Seeds 13

Back to the Earth 14

Glossary 15

Index 16

apple seed

Life Cycle Loops

Every living thing goes through a life cycle. Life cycles follow the changes in the life of a plant or animal. A plant begins life, grows, drops seeds, and dies. By dropping seeds, the plant starts the life cycle all over again.

The cycle is like a loop that happens over and over. Let's learn about the life cycle of an apple tree!

Starting as a Seed

Have you ever cut into an apple to see its seeds? They are hiding inside the fruit. All apple trees start as tiny seeds. The seeds have all the **nutrients** the tree needs to get started.

If the seed falls or is planted in rich soil, then it may start to sprout, or grow. Tiny roots reach down into the soil and the plant starts to push up out of the soil.

Sprout to Seedling

Sprouts grow tiny leaves. The leaves need sunlight so they can make food for the apple tree. If the plant gets enough sunlight and water, then it will start to grow taller.

Over time, the sprout turns into a seedling. Its stem becomes harder and taller. Its roots reach farther down into the ground. Its leaves grow so they can catch more sunlight.

Growing Taller

Seedlings turn into saplings if they have enough room to grow. Their stem becomes hard and starts to look more like bark. Now, the apple tree is on its way to becoming a mature, or adult, tree.

Adult trees grow **buds** in springtime. The buds then open into flowers. Honeybees come to the flowers and **pollinate** them. That makes new seeds.

Dropping Seeds

An apple forms around the seeds. The apple grows bigger in the summer and turns red or green. In fall, many apples become sweet and they're ready to be eaten.

People and animals eat apples that they pick from a tree or take from the ground. Animals scatter apple seeds in new places so more trees can grow. Some apples drop to the ground and rot, leaving seeds behind.

Back to the Earth

From a tiny apple seed, a new apple tree will grow. This starts the cycle all over again. In that way, the life cycle is like a loop.

Apple trees live on in another way, too. When the tree dies, it returns nutrients to the soil. From there, new apple trees or other plants may grow in its place. This life cycle loop happens for every apple tree you see!

Glossary

bud: A small growth on a plant's stem that becomes a flower, leaf, or new shoot.

nutrient: Something a living thing needs to grow and stay alive.

pollinate: To give a plant pollen from another plant of the same kind so seeds can be produced.

Index

A

apple tree, 5, 7, 9, 11, 14

L

leaves, 9

life cycle, 5, 14

loop, 5, 14

M

mature, 11

N

nutrient, 7

P

pollinate, 11

R

root, 7, 9

S

sapling, 11

seed, 4, 5, 7, 11, 13, 14

seedling, 9, 11

soil, 7, 14

sprout, 7, 9